ESTRANGED LOVE

HEALING THE WOUNDS OF A TROUBLED RELATIONSHIP

Becky Jaxon

Table of Content

Introduction: Understanding the Complexities of Relationship Problems

Once upon a time, I was in a relationship with someone I adored. However, I became alienated owing to a series of misunderstandings and miscommunications. I was upset and felt adrift without my loved one.

Despite my anguish and hurt, I did not give up on the relationship. I understood I still cared for my loved one and was determined to make things right. I stretched out, attempting to bridge the space between us, but was greeted with opposition.

Feeling dejected but not defeated, I chose to spend some time reflecting on myself and the acts that led to the estrangement. I recognized my errors and was eager to accept responsibility for them. I also learned that I needed to improve my communication skills and be more understanding of my loved one's emotions.

With this newfound knowledge, I attempted to reconcile with my loved one once again. I approached the subject this time with honesty, vulnerability, and a readiness to listen. To my surprise and relief, my loved one was eager to hear me out and work on the relationship as well.

It was not an easy route to reconciliation. There were still misunderstandings and arguments, but I and my loved one were determined to work things out. We made a concerted effort to communicate more effectively and comprehend one another's points of view. We also made time for one another and prioritized our relationship.

I and my loved one were able to reestablish our connection through persistence and devotion to one another. We rediscovered pleasure and love. I was glad for the lessons I had learned as well as the opportunity to restart our relationship. I realized it was worthwhile to battle for something I cared about.

Relationships are complicated and multifaceted, and it may be difficult to know where to turn or what to do when issues occur. Whether its communication challenges, conflict, trust issues, or something else, the problems that afflict relationships are frequently deeply ingrained and difficult to resolve. Understanding the intricacies of relationship difficulties, on the other hand, is the first step toward resolving them and building a stronger, more rewarding relationship.

Poor communication is one of the most prevalent reasons for relationship issues. When partners do not feel heard or understood, they may experience irritation, anger, and detachment. Furthermore, misunderstandings and disagreements might arise when partners do not know how to communicate themselves clearly and assertively. Poor communication may also lead to feelings of isolation and loneliness, as couples begin to emotionally distance themselves from one another.

A lack of trust is another typical source of relationship issues. Trust is the cornerstone of every successful relationship, and it may be difficult to feel comfortable or confident in the relationship if it is lacking. Infidelity, dishonesty, or just a lack of closeness and connection may all lead to trust difficulties. When trust is shattered, it is tough to reestablish, and the relationship may never recover completely.

Another important source of marital issues is conflict. While some amount of disagreement is typical in every relationship, when arguments become chronic or are not adequately handled, they may hurt the partnership. Chronic disagreement may cause sentiments of resentment, wrath, and frustration, eventually leading to a breakdown in communication and trust.

Another big source of marital issues is infidelity. When one partner cheats on the other, the relationship might suffer greatly. Infidelity may elicit sentiments of rage, betrayal, and pain, making it difficult to move on and regain trust.

Aside from these frequent reasons for relationship issues, a variety of additional circumstances may also contribute to relationship troubles. A lack of closeness and connection, for example, might result in emotions of isolation and loneliness, whilst a lack of boundaries can result in feelings of suffocation and resentment.

Understanding the intricacies of relationship difficulties, on the other hand, is merely the first step toward addressing them. It is also necessary to acquire good communication skills, establish trust and intimacy, and learn how to successfully handle disagreements to form a solid and enduring relationship. You may empower yourself to establish a stronger, more meaningful relationship by taking the time to grasp the nuances of relationship difficulties and acquiring the skills and methods to overcome them.

Finally, since relationships are complicated and multifaceted, it may be difficult to know where to turn or what to do when issues develop. Understanding the intricacies of relationship difficulties, on the other hand, is the first step toward resolving them and building a stronger, more rewarding relationship. Whether you're dealing with communication challenges, conflict, trust issues, or anything else, the goal is to identify and address the underlying reasons for the problem. You can empower yourself to establish a better, more rewarding relationship with the correct tools and tactics.

Chapter 1: Identifying the Root Causes of Relationship Issues

Relationship problems may be complicated and multifaceted, resulting from a range of variables such as individual psychological and emotional elements as well as social and cultural ones.

However, the following are some probable fundamental reasons of relationship problems that might be discussed:

Poor communication is one of the most prevalent reasons of relationship issues. Misunderstandings and misinterpretations may develop when partners are unable to adequately express their needs, emotions, and opinions. This may lead to disagreements, animosity, and the breakup of the partnership. Furthermore, a lack of efficient communication makes it difficult for partners to comprehend and support one another, leading to feelings of isolation and detachment.

Unsolved past problems: Past traumas or unresolved difficulties from previous relationships might influence how people interact with their present partners. For example, if a person has been harmed in a past relationship, they may have trust difficulties, making it harder for them to completely open up to their present spouse. Furthermore, unresolved past difficulties may leave people with emotional baggage that affects how they process and react to present relationship dynamics.

Differences in values and objectives: It may be difficult for partners to establish common ground and develop a successful relationship when they have distinct values, goals, and priorities. If one couple prioritizes job progress while the other prioritizes home and children, this might lead to tensions and misunderstandings. Furthermore, when partners have opposing aims and priorities, making choices and planning for the future may be challenging.

Lack of trust and commitment: Trust and commitment are needed for a good relationship, and a lack of either may lead to adultery, emotional distancing, and relationship dissolution. When trust is lacking, couples may experience emotions of uneasiness and jealousy. Furthermore, when there is a lack of commitment, partners may be concerned about the relationship's future.

Individual emotional and psychological concerns, such as anxiety, sadness, and attachment disorders, may have an impact on how a person interacts with their spouse. Someone suffering from anxiety, for example, may battle with trust difficulties, making it difficult for them to completely open up to their spouse. Furthermore, someone suffering from depression may have thoughts of despair, which might impair their capacity to participate in the relationship.

Society and cultural variables, such as gender norms and societal expectations, may also play a part in relationship problems. For example, cultural expectations about gender roles might influence how people perceive and behave in relationships. Furthermore, cultural and religious beliefs might impact how people see and approach relationships.

It's crucial to remember that these are only a few instances of probable underlying causes of relationship problems, and that every relationship is different. It's also worth noting that many of these variables may combine and intensify each other, making it difficult to identify and manage the underlying difficulties.

Common causes of relationship problems

There are several frequent reasons for relationship troubles, and they vary based on the relationship and the persons involved. Among the most prevalent reasons are:

1. **Communication problems**: In a relationship, poor communication may show in a variety of ways. When one partner expresses their views or worries, they may not feel heard or understood. Frustration, alienation, and anger may result from this. Furthermore, when problems emerge, if the partners do not know how to successfully communicate, they may avoid addressing the issue or use

nasty or angry words, which may exacerbate the situation.

2. **Trust issues**: Trust is essential in every good relationship. It gives both parties a sense of security and confidence in their relationship. When trust is shattered, it may be tough to repair the connection. If one spouse is unfaithful or lies to the other, it may cause emotions of uneasiness, jealousy, and betrayal. These sentiments may be tough to overcome, making it harder for the relationship to progress.
3. **Financial issues**: Money is often a cause of stress and strain in relationships. This might involve conflicts over spending patterns, differences in financial objectives

or one spouse feeling as though they bear the bulk of the financial load. For instance, if one spouse is more financially responsible than the other, he or she may feel resentful or stressed. This might cause disagreements and make it harder for the partnership to grow.

Intimacy is an essential component of every love connection. Physical, emotional, and intellectual closeness are all part of it. When one or both partners are dissatisfied or feel detached in this area, it may lead to feelings of loneliness and discontent. If one spouse is not interested in physical closeness, the other may feel rejected or irrelevant. This might cause a schism between the couples, making it harder for the partnership to flourish.

1. **Different expectations**: When one spouse has different expectations than the other, relationships may become troublesome. Differences in lifestyle, beliefs or long-term aspirations are examples of this. For example, if one couple wants to settle down and establish a family but the other partner is not ready, stress and conflict might arise. If these discrepancies in expectations are not addressed and resolved, the relationship may struggle to proceed.
2. **Lack of compromise**: Compromise is vital in every relationship. When one

spouse refuses to compromise or meet the other halfway, it may lead to anger and dissatisfaction. For example, if one spouse consistently makes all of the choices, the other may feel ignored or irrelevant. This might cause a schism between the couples, making it harder for the partnership to flourish.

3. **Infidelity**: Cheating may be a major source of relationship troubles. It may lead to emotions of betrayal, pain, and resentment, making it harder for the relationship to heal. A spouse who has been cheated on may experience a variety of feelings, including anger, sadness, and betrayal. These sentiments may be tough to

overcome, making it harder for the relationship to progress.

4. **Lack of common values**: When two individuals have conflicting ideals, it might be difficult for them to comprehend one another. For example, if one couple emphasizes job success while the other loves family, their priorities may diverge, causing friction and conflict.
5. **Lack of commitment**: For any relationship to flourish, commitment is required. Without it, one partner may feel unvalued or unappreciated, leading to feelings of uneasiness and unhappiness. For example, if one spouse is unwilling to prioritize the relationship, the other may

feel ignored or irrelevant. This might cause a schism between the couples, making it harder for the partnership to flourish.

6. **Power disparities**: When one person has more authority or control in the relationship, the other partner may experience resentment and irritation. This may present itself in a variety of ways, such as one person making all of the choices, dominating, or dismissing the other partner's thoughts and emotions. This may generate a feeling of inequity in the connection, making it harder for it to flourish.

Past traumas might interfere with a person's capacity to build and sustain good relationships.

It may lead to trust concerns, intimacy challenges, and communication difficulties. For example, if one spouse was abused as a kid, they may have difficulty trusting people or allowing themselves to be vulnerable. This might make it harder for them to build deep bonds and cause issues in their relationship.

7. **Lack of common interests**: Having shared interests and hobbies in a relationship may give a feeling of closeness and shared experiences. When couples have opposing interests, it may be difficult to establish common ground and produce emotions of distance and separation. For example, if one couple enjoys sports but

the other does not, it may be difficult for them to find things to do together.

8. **Interference from family**: Interference from family may be a key source of relationship troubles. When one partner's family becomes unduly engaged in the relationship, tension and conflict might arise. For example, if one partner's family is always offering unwanted advice or attempting to exert control over the relationship, it may make it difficult for the pair to make their own choices and build distance between the partners.
9. **Personal development**: As people grow and evolve, their needs and priorities may shift. If the partners are unable to adjust

and support one other's progress, this might cause issues in the relationship. For example, if one spouse wants to pursue a new job or hobby and the other partner is unsupportive, stress and conflict might arise.

Overall, relationships are complicated and may be influenced by a variety of variables. It is important to be aware of the possible reasons for relationship difficulties and to collaborate to address and overcome any issues that may occur. Communication, trust, compromise, and a willingness to work through challenges are all essential for a happy and successful relationship.

How to recognize the signs of a failing relationship

Recognizing the indications of a failing relationship may be challenging since issues are frequently subtle and not immediately apparent. However, it is important to be aware of the warning signals so that you can treat any problems before they worsen. Here are some warning signals that your relationship is in trouble:

Communication breakdown: One of the most prevalent indications of a failed relationship is a communication breakdown. If you and your spouse are no longer communicating freely and honestly with each other, it might indicate that your relationship is in peril. This might appear in several ways, such as one spouse emotionally closing down, avoiding uncomfortable talks, or refusing to communicate their ideas and emotions.

Lack of intimacy: Physical and emotional closeness are equally crucial aspects of any relationship. If you and your spouse are no longer physically or emotionally close to each other, this might indicate that your relationship is in peril. This may present itself in a multitude of ways, such as one spouse avoiding physical contact or refusing to discuss their ideas and emotions.

Lack of trust: Trust is a critical component of every good relationship. If you and your spouse no longer trust one other, this might indicate that your relationship is in peril. This may take many forms, including one partner becoming suspicious or envious, or refusing to disclose personal information.

Constant arguing and fighting: Another clue that a relationship is in peril is constant bickering and fighting. If you and your spouse are continually bickering and fighting, it may indicate that underlying problems need to be addressed. This may take many forms, such as one spouse being critical or dismissive of the other, or refusing to listen or compromise.

Lack of common objectives and values: Every partnership must have shared goals and values. If you and your spouse no longer share the same objectives and values, this might indicate that your relationship is in peril. This may show itself in several ways, such as one spouse desiring different goals in life or being unable to agree on major topics.

Support is an essential component of every good relationship. If you and your spouse are no longer supportive of one another, it might indicate that your relationship is in peril. This may show in several ways, such as one spouse refusing to assist the other with work or being emotionally unavailable to them.

Respect: Respect is an essential component of every good relationship. If you and your spouse are no longer respectful of each other, this might indicate that your relationship is in peril. This may present itself in several ways, such as one spouse dismissing or criticizing the other, or refusing to listen or compromise.

Lack of commitment: Commitment is essential in any good relationship. If you and your spouse are no longer dedicated to the relationship, this might indicate that it is in peril. This may show in a lot of ways, such as one spouse being more focused on other things or being unwilling to put out the effort required to make the relationship work.

Lack of passion: In every healthy relationship, passion is essential. If you and your lover are no longer enthralled by one other, it might indicate that your relationship is in peril. This may present itself in a lot of ways, such as one spouse becoming less interested in physical intimacy or being less affectionate or loving than they used to be.

Constant negative sentiments, such as anger, resentment, or sadness, might also indicate that a relationship is in peril. If you are continually having bad feelings toward your spouse, or if your partner is frequently expressing negative emotions toward you, it may indicate that there are underlying difficulties in the relationship that need to be addressed.

It's important to note that some of the following symptoms are natural and may occur in any relationship. It is also possible to have a nice and healthy relationship without experiencing all of the aforementioned benefits. If you see some of the above indications in your relationship, it may be good talking to your spouse about how you both feel and what measures you may take to resolve any concerns.

To repair a broken relationship, it is necessary to first address the underlying issues that are generating the difficulties. This may need some introspection and open dialogue with your spouse. It is also important to seek expert assistance if you believe you are unable to handle the difficulties on your own. A therapist or counselor may assist you and your relationship in overcoming obstacles and developing good communication and problem-solving abilities.

It's also crucial to understand that relationships don't always work out, despite our best attempts. If you've done everything and still feel that the relationship isn't healthy or rewarding, it may be time to call it quits. In every relationship, remember to take care of yourself and prioritize your well-being.

In conclusion, identifying the indicators of a deteriorating relationship is critical so that you may address any problems before they worsen. Lack of communication, closeness, trust, continual bickering and fighting, lack of shared objectives and ideals, lack of support, lack of respect, lack of commitment, lack of enthusiasm, and persistent unpleasant sentiments are some typical indications. If you see multiple of these indications in your relationship, it may be time to talk to your spouse about how you both feel and what measures you may take to resolve any concerns.

Chapter 2: Communicating Effectively in a Relationship

Effective communication is a fundamental component of a healthy relationship. To communicate well in a relationship, both parties must be able to express their views, emotions, and wants clearly and freely, while also being able to listen actively and empathetically to the other person.

One crucial part of good communication is the capacity to explain oneself simply and directly. This implies being able to explain one's ideas, emotions, and desires in a manner that is simple for the other person to grasp. It also implies being able to talk in a calm and non-judgmental way, avoiding blame or criticism.

Another crucial part of good communication is active listening. This implies being present and involved in the discussion and giving the other person your whole attention. It also involves being able to comprehend the other person's viewpoint, even if you don't agree with it.

Effective communication also involves the capacity to be open and honest with one another. This includes being willing to discuss your ideas, emotions, and wants with your spouse, even though it may be difficult or unpleasant to do so. It also involves being willing to listen to your partner's opinions, emotions, and wants, even if you don't agree with them.

In addition to these fundamental communication skills, there are a few additional crucial tactics that may assist to increase communication in a partnership. For example, it might be good to set up regular "communication time" to chat with your spouse about significant concerns and to check in with each other about how things are doing in the relationship.

Another key tactic is to be open to compromise and negotiation. This involves being willing to find a middle ground and making sacrifices to create a solution that works for both parties.

It's also crucial to be aware of and regulate your emotions. When we're feeling unhappy, it might be tough to communicate properly. It's vital to take a step back, take a deep breath and restore your composure before participating in a discussion.

One crucial part of good verbal communication is the usage of "I" statements. Instead of casting accusations or putting blame, adopting "I" statements helps one to convey their thoughts and needs in a non-threatening manner. For example, instead of expressing "You never listen to me," one may say "I feel like I'm not being heard."

Active listening is also a crucial part of good verbal communication. This entails not just paying attention to what the other person is saying, but also making an effort to grasp their viewpoint, emotions, and needs. This may be done by tactics such as reflecting on what the other person has said, asking clarifying questions, and summarizing the important aspects of the discussion.

Nonverbal communication also plays a key part in good communication in a relationship. This encompasses body language, facial expressions, tone of voice, and physical contact. For example, keeping eye contact and a relaxed posture might show attention and openness, whereas crossing arms or avoiding eye contact can suggest defensiveness or closed-mindedness.

It's also crucial to be aware of and handle conflict healthily. This includes learning to communicate disagreement and constructively settle problems, rather than becoming defensive or violent. Techniques such as compromise, negotiation, and pursuing a win-win solution may be effective in handling conflict.

Effective communication also demands the capacity to apologize and forgive. This entails accepting responsibility for one's acts and apologizing when appropriate, as well as being able to forgive and move on from previous errors.

Another crucial method for efficient communication is to create regular "conversation time" with your spouse. This may be a regular time each week when you can address significant topics and check in with each other about how things are doing in the relationship. This may also assist avoid tiny difficulties from becoming major ones.

In addition, successful communication entails being able to empathize with your partner's emotions, ideas, and wants. This involves understanding and being able to empathize with their sentiments even if you don't agree with them. It also involves being able to put oneself in their shoes and knowing how they may feel in a specific circumstance.

Lastly, good communication in a relationship needs both parties to be willing to improve on communication skills. This includes being open to comments, eager to learn and develop, and actively striving to enhance communication in the partnership.

Additionally, it's crucial to be conscious of your body language and tone of voice while speaking. Facial expressions, gestures, and tone of voice may convey a lot about how you're feeling and can be a strong tool for expressing yourself.

Lastly, it's crucial to remember that communication is a two-way path. Both parties must be willing to put in the effort to communicate properly for the relationship to be successful. It's crucial to work together to enhance communication and to be patient and understanding with one another as you attempt to establish stronger communication skills.

In summary, efficient communication is a critical component of a healthy relationship. It requires the ability to express oneself clearly and directly, to listen actively and empathetically, to be open and honest, to set aside regular communication time, to be willing to compromise and negotiate, to be aware of and manage emotions, to be aware of body language and tone of voice and lastly both partners must be willing to put in the effort to communicate effectively.

The importance of active listening and empathy

Active listening and empathy are both necessary for creating and sustaining successful relationships.

Active listening is the practice of completely paying attention to and comprehending what the other person is saying, both orally and non-verbally. This means not just hearing the words people are speaking, but also comprehending the underlying meaning and feelings behind them. By carefully listening, you may obtain a better knowledge of your partner's viewpoint and emotions, which can lead to increased closeness and connection in the relationship.

There are various essential parts to active listening, including:

- Giving your whole attention to the other person, without interruptions.
- Reflecting on what the other person has said, indicates that you have comprehended and are paying attention.
- Asking clarifying questions, to ensure that you have a clear comprehension of what the other person is saying.
- Summarizing the essential elements of the talk, to ensure that you are on the same page.
- Active listening also entails being present at the moment and not simply thinking about what you will say next. It also includes not interrupting or talking over

your spouse, and not getting defensive or dismissive of their sentiments.

Empathy is the capacity to comprehend and share the sentiments of another person. It entails being able to put yourself in their shoes and comprehend how they may feel in a specific scenario, even if you don't agree with them. Empathy is vital for creating trust and closeness in a relationship since it helps to generate a deeper understanding and connection between partners.

There are various fundamental factors to empathy, including:

Being able to comprehend and empathize with the other person's sentiments, even if you don't agree with them.

Being able to recognize and accept the other person's sentiments, without criticizing or discarding them.

Being able to convey that you understand and support the other person's sentiments.

Empathy also demands being able to listen attentively and grasp the other person's viewpoint, even if it is different from your own. It also involves being able to manage your own emotions and behaviors, so that you can be present and supportive of your spouse.

Active listening and empathy are both needed for good communication in a partnership. By actively listening and demonstrating empathy, partners may get a better knowledge of each other's viewpoints and emotions, which can lead to greater closeness and connection in the relationship.

Active listening and empathy also play a vital role in resolving disputes and managing differences healthily. When couples actively listen and demonstrate empathy towards each other, they are more likely to discover common ground and come to a conclusion that works for both of them.

Active listening and empathy also assist to create trust and closeness in a relationship. When partners feel heard and understood, they are more inclined to trust and open up to each other, which may lead to deeper intimacy and connection.

Both active listening and empathy also involve self-awareness and emotional intelligence. It involves being aware of your own emotions, thoughts, and responses and being able to manage them in a manner that enables you to be present for your partner.

In summary, active listening and empathy are both crucial for creating and sustaining successful relationships. Active listening entails paying attention and comprehending what the other person is saying, whereas empathy involves being able to understand and share the sentiments of another person. Both active listening and empathy are crucial for efficient communication, resolving problems and managing disagreements, creating trust and closeness in a partnership. Both also involve self-awareness and emotional intelligence.

How to express yourself clearly and assertively

In a relationship, being able to express oneself clearly and assertively is a vital ability for sustaining good communication and resolving issues. It entails being open about one's thoughts and wants while also being respectful of and sympathetic to the other person's point of view.

Being able to properly explain one's requirements and limits is an important part of clear and forceful communication. This includes being able to convey what one wants and does not want, as well as saying "no" when required. It also entails being able to express one's sentiments and emotions openly, rather than burying them or being passive-aggressive.

Another crucial part of assertive communication is the ability to attentively listen to the other person's point of view. This entails being attentive and interested in the discourse rather than getting defensive or dismissive. It also entails being able to think back on what the other person has said to ensure that you comprehend their point of view.

It is also vital to employ "I" statements rather than "you" statements when expressing oneself clearly and assertively. This indicates that you should convey your thoughts and needs rather than criticize or accuse the other person. Instead of stating, "You never listen to me," you may add, "When you don't listen to me, I feel wounded and disrespected."

Maintaining eye contact, speaking in a calm and steady tone of voice, and standing or sitting up straight are all examples of forceful body language. Avoid crossing your arms or slouching, which might create the appearance that you are defensive or closed off.

Another important part of assertive communication is the ability to establish and maintain limits. This includes being able to say "no" when required and enforcing such limits when they are violated. It also entails being able to respect the other person's limits and not pressuring them to do anything they do not want to do.

Here are some more tips for expressing oneself clearly and assertively in a relationship:

Be particular and explicit: It's important to be specific and clear about what you want when communicating your sentiments and desires. This implies avoiding unclear or imprecise language in favor of specific language that clearly expresses your meaning. Instead of stating "I'm wounded," you may say "I'm hurt when you don't call me when you're going to be late." This will help the other person understand what you need and how they can assist you.

As previously stated, employing "I" statements is a key element of assertive communication. This indicates that you should convey your thoughts and needs rather than criticize or accuse the other person. This may keep the other person from feeling defensive and make it simpler for them to comprehend and react to your requirements.

Practice active listening: Active listening is an important part of forceful communication. This entails being attentive and interested in the discourse rather than getting defensive or dismissive. It also entails being able to think back on what the other person has said to ensure that you comprehend their point of view.

Active listening contributes to the development of trust and understanding in a relationship.

Establish and maintain limits: It is critical to establish and maintain boundaries in a relationship. This includes being able to say "no" when required and enforcing such limits when they are violated. It also entails being able to respect the other person's limits and not pressuring them to do anything they do not want to do. Setting limits is essential for keeping a good balance in the relationship and ensuring that the needs of both parties are satisfied.

Use aggressive body language: Your body language may have a significant impact on how you seem while talking. Maintaining eye contact, speaking in a calm and steady tone of voice, and standing or sitting up straight are all examples of forceful body language. Avoid crossing your arms or slouching, which might create the appearance that you are defensive or closed off.

Take responsibility for your actions: It is critical in assertive communication to accept responsibility for your acts and emotions. This entails admitting your part in the event and not blaming the other person. Taking responsibility for your actions may help to defuse confrontations and make finding a solution simpler.

Empathy is the capacity to comprehend and share the emotions of another person. It's critical in a relationship to cultivate empathy and attempt to see things from the other person's point of view. This may aid in the development of understanding and trust, making it simpler to settle problems.

Use "assertive" communication instead of "aggressive" or "passive" communication: A good blend of aggressive and passive communication is assertive communication. It entails being able to communicate your wants plainly and bluntly while still being courteous and understanding of the other person's point of view. Aggressive communication often entails accusing and assaulting the other person, while passive communication involves avoiding confrontation and failing to advocate for oneself.

It's also crucial to remember that communication is a two-way street, and both people in a relationship should be ready to work on improving their communication skills. It might take time to build clear and forceful communication skills, so be patient with yourself and your spouse while you work on strengthening your communication. Finally, in a relationship, it is critical to cultivating empathy and understanding. This entails being able to put oneself in the shoes of another person and perceive things from their point of view. It also entails being able to recognize and acknowledge the sentiments of others, even if you disagree with them.

To summarize, being able to express oneself clearly and assertively in a relationship requires a mix of good communication skills, empathy, and the capacity to create and keep limits. Individuals may enhance their communication in a relationship and develop better and healthier relationships by being honest and courteous, actively listening, employing "I" statements, using forceful body language, and exercising empathy.

Chapter 3: Resolving Conflicts in a Relationship

Resolving disagreements in a relationship may be difficult, but it is necessary for the partnership's health and durability. Conflicts may occur from several factors, including differences in beliefs, communication styles, and life objectives. The key to settling problems is to approach them with an open mind and a readiness to compromise, rather than with a defensive stance.

The first stage in conflict resolution is determining the root of the problem. Taking a step back and looking at the issue objectively, rather than getting caught up in the emotions of the moment, may be necessary. Once the root of the issue has been discovered, it is critical to discuss your thoughts and concerns with your spouse openly and honestly.

Conflict resolution requires effective communication. It is critical to convey your sentiments using "I" words rather than "you" phrases. Instead of expressing, "You usually do this," try, "I feel wounded when you do this." This prevents you from blaming your spouse and enables them to realize how your behaviors affect you.

When settling problems, active listening is also essential. This is listening to and comprehending what your spouse is saying without interrupting or getting defensive.

Allowing your spouse to share their thoughts and worries without interruption or judgment is critical.

After all, sides have had an opportunity to vent their thoughts, it is time to develop conflict resolution strategies. It is critical to find solutions that address all sides' demands and concerns. Compromise is essential in conflict resolution, and it is critical to be open to other options that may not fully fit with your desires.

It is also critical to set and respect limits in the partnership. This implies that everyone should be able to establish limitations and make decisions about their own needs and well-being. When disagreements emerge, it is critical to respect each other's limits and collaborate to find a mutually beneficial solution.

Another important part of conflict resolution is accepting responsibility for your actions and feelings. This entails being honest with yourself about your involvement in the disagreement and being willing to adjust your behavior to better the situation.

In addition to these tactics, seeking outside aid when resolving issues in a relationship might be beneficial. A therapist or counselor may help you work through difficulties and develop your communication and problem-solving abilities.

Here is some extra information to assist you in better understand and using the conflict resolution tactics in a relationship:

Managing Emotions: It is important to know that during confrontations, emotions may run high, making it difficult to remain calm and reasonable. One good method is to take a pause and allow yourself to calm down before resuming the conversation. This enables you to approach the argument with a more level-headed and sensible perspective. To assist regulate your emotions during disagreements, you may also try strategies like deep breathing or mindfulness.

Finding Common Ground: When problems emerge, it is important to establish common ground with your spouse to discover solutions that benefit both of you. Begin by determining the underlying wants and concerns that are creating the disagreement. If you're battling over money, for example, the underlying need might be a need for financial stability. You may work together to discover a solution that answers both of your concerns by recognizing this shared need.

Empathy: Expressing empathy for your partner's point of view may assist to foster a feeling of understanding and connection. This is attempting to see things through your partner's eyes and accepting and supporting their sentiments. This may assist to reduce stress and create a more pleasant and productive atmosphere for dispute resolution.

Using a "Softened Beginning": A softened startup is a technique for bringing up a difficult issue or worry without putting your partner on the defensive. This may be accomplished by speaking in a friendly, non-confrontational tone and beginning with a positive comment or inquiry. Instead of stating, "You never assist me with the housework," you may add, "I was wondering if we could discuss how we can share the chores more equitably."

Using a "Time-Out": A "time-out" is a method of taking a break from an argument when it becomes too hot. This might be accomplished by simply taking a little break or by agreeing to return to the subject at a later time. It is critical to avoid discussing or attempting to settle the disagreement during a time-out. Instead, concentrate on relaxing and recovering your composure.

Apologizing and Forgiving: Apologizing and forgiving are critical parts of dispute resolution. Apologizing allows one to accept responsibility for one's actions and express regret while forgiving allows one to let go of animosity and move on from the issue. It is important to remember that apologies and forgiveness must be sincere.

Being Willing to Seek Help: In certain circumstances, disputes may be too tough to settle on your own, necessitating the assistance of a therapist or counselor. A therapist can guide and encourage you while you work through difficulties, as well as assist you and your spouse improve your communication and problem-solving abilities.

You may increase your capacity to manage disagreements healthily and effectively by applying these tactics. Remember that resolving problems requires time, patience, and practice. You may develop your relationship and establish a stronger connection with your spouse through open conversation and active listening, mutual respect, and dedication to finding mutually beneficial solutions and obtaining professional assistance if necessary. To summarize, conflict resolution in a relationship requires a desire to understand and compromise, good communication, active listening, mutual respect, and a commitment to finding mutually beneficial solutions. It is critical to approach disagreements with optimism and to accept responsibility for your actions and emotions. With these skills and tactics, you can handle disagreements healthily and successfully, while also strengthening your relationship with your spouse.

Strategies for effective conflict resolution

i. **Communication:** Effective communication is the basis of every healthy relationship, particularly when it comes to dispute resolution. Being open and honest about your thoughts and worries with your spouse might help to avoid arguments from growing. It's also important to actively listen to your spouse and attempt to grasp their point of view.

It is critical to employ "I" statements rather than "you" comments while talking during a quarrel. This might help you avoid blaming your spouse and make it simpler for you to share your thoughts and worries. Avoid using accusing, judgemental, or hostile language. Instead, utilize words that reflect your sentiments and worries in a non-threatening and peaceful manner.

It's also vital not to interrupt your partner while they're speaking and to let them complete their idea before answering. This may aid in making both parties feel heard and understood.

ii. **Problem-Solving**: When disagreements emerge, it is critical to stay focused on the issue at hand and collaborate to find a solution. This may include brainstorming many ideas, assessing the advantages and drawbacks of each, and arriving at a compromise that both parties are satisfied with.

It is critical to approach problem-solving with an open mind and a desire to understand the other person's point of view. It's also important to remain patient and avoid jumping to conclusions. It may take some time to discover the appropriate answer, but it will be worthwhile in the end.

iii. **Empathy**: Putting yourself in your partner's shoes and attempting to comprehend their point of view may be a significant strategy in dispute resolution. Empathy fosters trust and understanding between couples, making it simpler to discover common ground.

When attempting to comprehend your partner's point of view, it is critical to ask questions and show real attention in their responses. Make no assumptions or leap to conclusions. Instead, attempt to comprehend their sentiments and worries by seeing things from their perspective.

iv. **Maintain your cool**: When disagreements develop, it is easy to get caught up in the moment and say or do things we later regret. It is critical to maintain your cool and avoid becoming defensive or confrontational. This may assist to deescalate the issue and make finding a solution simpler.

Before reacting, it is critical to take a deep breath and count to 10. This might help you collect your thoughts and reply in a calm, calculated manner. It's also vital to avoid using harsh language or raising your voice. Instead, use a steady, even tone of voice.

v. **Take a break**: Taking a break from the disagreement might be beneficial at times. This allows both parties to calm down and reflect on the issue more clearly. Setting a time to return to the topic and finish the dialogue is also a good idea.

It's critical to set clear limits and give each other space while taking a vacation. It's also critical not to use the break as an excuse to escape the issue entirely. Instead, use this time to collect your ideas and prepare for a productive dialogue.

vi. **Professional assistance**: If disagreements reoccur and cannot be handled by the couple, it may be beneficial to seek the assistance of a professional therapist or counselor. A professional may assist in mediating the discussion and providing skills and strategies for successful communication and conflict resolution.

A therapist may assist in identifying underlying problems that may be contributing to the disputes and can give assistance and support in resolving these difficulties. They may also offer the couple skills and tactics for better communication and conflict resolution.

vii. **Determine the source of the conflict**: It is critical to treat the fundamental source of the dispute rather than merely the symptoms. This may aid in the prevention of such confrontations in the future.

For example, if a marriage is fighting about money, it might be because one spouse feels unheard or disrespected when it comes to financial matters. If a couple is fighting over spending time together, one spouse may be feeling ignored or unsupported in other aspects of the relationship.

Couples may address the underlying problems and strive toward a settlement that tackles the true problem rather than merely treating the symptoms by recognizing the main cause of the disagreement.

viii. **Show appreciation and thanks**: Expressing gratitude and appreciation to your spouse may assist to establish a pleasant environment in the relationship, making it simpler to overcome problems.

It might assist to create trust and understanding when you recognize and recognize your partner's contributions to the relationship. It may also aid in the development of mutual respect and the strengthening of the couple's relationship.

ix. **Be willing to compromise**: A strong relationship requires compromise. To create a solution that works for both parties, you must be prepared to compromise.

Compromise does not imply giving up what you want or need, but it does include being prepared to make sacrifices and find a solution that meets both parties requirements.

- **Forgiveness should be practiced**: Forgiveness is an essential component of every good relationship. When disputes develop, it is critical to be able to forgive your spouse and move on from the past.

Forgiveness does not imply forgetting what occurred or justifying poor conduct; rather, it entails letting go of anger and resentment and finding a means to move ahead. This may assist to maintain a pleasant relationship environment and avoid problems from growing.

To summarize, effective conflict resolution in relationships necessitates open and honest communication, problem-solving, empathy, calmness, taking a break, professional assistance, identifying the root cause, expressing appreciation and gratitude, being willing to compromise, and practicing forgiveness.

Issues are a natural part of every relationship, and with the correct tools and strategy, couples can work through conflicts and establish a stronger, better connection.

How to avoid common pitfalls in conflict management

Conflict resolution in relationships may be difficult, and there are numerous typical problems that couples might encounter.

Couples may enhance their capacity to successfully settle problems and establish a better, healthier relationship by being aware of these dangers and learning how to avoid them.

Avoiding or denying the conflict: Avoiding or denying the problem is one of the most prevalent errors in conflict resolution. Couples who ignore or deny problems are not addressing the underlying causes, which may result in unresolved disagreements and animosity.

Couples must be honest with one another and admit when disagreements emerge. Couples may strive toward a settlement by confronting difficulties front on and being ready to have open and honest dialogues.

Blaming and attacking: Blaming and attacking is another prevalent problem in conflict resolution. Couples who blame and attack one other are not focused on resolving the dispute. Instead, they are concerned with assigning blame and making the other person feel guilty or defensive.

Couples must accept responsibility for their behaviors and concentrate on finding a solution rather than assigning blame. This may be accomplished by utilizing "I" words and concentrating on how you feel instead of making accusations.

Becoming defensive: Another typical error in dispute resolution is being defensive. When partners get defensive, they are not listening to the other person's point of view, which makes it harder to reach an agreement.

It is critical for partners to be open to hearing the other person's point of view and to be prepared to consider it. Couples may work toward a solution that meets the requirements of both parties by being honest and ready to listen.

Ignoring emotions: Another typical error in dispute resolution is ignoring feelings. Couples who disregard their feelings are failing to address the underlying emotions that are fueling the dispute. Unresolved disagreements and anger might result from this.

Couples must be aware of their own emotions and ready to express them healthily. Couples may strive toward a settlement that addresses the underlying emotions by admitting and addressing feelings.

Another typical error in dispute resolution is the failure to establish limits. Couples who do not create boundaries are not establishing clear expectations for how their relationship should work. This might lead to disagreements and misunderstandings.

Couples must establish clear limits and convey them to one another. Couples may foster mutual respect and understanding by establishing limits.

Another major error in dispute resolution is the failure to seek expert assistance. When couples do not seek professional counseling, they are not gaining an objective view of the problem, which may make finding a settlement difficult.

When disagreements become too tough to settle on their own, couples should seek expert counseling. A therapist or counselor may assist couples in identifying and resolving underlying difficulties.

In summary, frequent mistakes in relationship conflict management include avoiding or denying the problem, blaming and attacking, being defensive, disregarding emotions, failing to create boundaries, and failing to seek professional assistance. Couples may enhance their capacity to successfully settle problems and establish a better, healthier relationship by being aware of these dangers and learning how to avoid them. It's vital to remember that disagreements are natural, and how we manage them may make or destroy a relationship.

Chapter 4: Building Trust and Intimacy in a Relationship

Building trust and closeness in a relationship are critical for developing a strong, healthy bond with your spouse. Trust and intimacy are inextricably linked, and both are required for a relationship to flourish. In this post, we will look at many ways for increasing trust and closeness in a relationship.

Communicate freely and honestly: Open and honest communication is one of the most critical components in developing trust and closeness. When partners feel comfortable sharing their ideas and emotions without fear of being judged or rejected, they develop a greater degree of trust and intimacy.

It is critical to provide a secure and non-judgmental atmosphere for discourse to develop open and honest communication. This may be accomplished by making time for chatting, selecting the appropriate time and location, and being courteous and listening while the other person is speaking.

Be constant and dependable: Building trust in a relationship requires consistency and reliability. When partners can depend on each other to be there for them, they generate a feeling of security, which is necessary for creating trust.

To be consistent and dependable, you must follow through on pledges and commitments, be dependable in times of need, and be emotionally and physically present for your spouse.

Share vulnerabilities and be vulnerable: Trust and intimacy are inextricably linked to the capacity to share weaknesses and be vulnerable to the vulnerabilities of others. When couples can communicate their concerns, anxieties, and inadequacies with one another, trust and closeness grow.

To disclose vulnerabilities and be open to others' weaknesses, it is necessary, to be honest about your vulnerabilities, to be supportive and nonjudgmental when your partner discusses their flaws, and to work together to remedy any vulnerabilities that occur in the relationship.

Show appreciation and thankfulness: Another crucial component in developing trust and closeness in a relationship is to express appreciation and thanks. When couples feel valued and respected, it fosters greater trust and closeness.

It is crucial to communicate your thoughts of appreciation and gratitude frequently, to be particular in your statements of appreciation, and to demonstrate your appreciation via deeds as well as words.

Work on conflict resolution: Conflicts that are not addressed successfully may harm trust and closeness. Conflicts that are not adequately addressed may lead to emotions of anger and detachment, which can destroy trust and closeness.

To successfully settle disputes, it is necessary to employ strong communication skills, concentrate on finding solutions rather than assigning blame, and be prepared to compromise and negotiate.

Physical affection is a crucial part of developing trust and closeness in a relationship. Physical contact fosters a feeling of connection and bonding, which is necessary for developing trust and intimacy.

To demonstrate physical affection, it is necessary to be loving and to initiate physical contact regularly. Hugs, kisses, holding hands, and snuggling are all examples of this.

Share experiences and create shared memories: Another crucial aspect in developing trust and closeness in a relationship is sharing experiences and creating shared memories. When couples share experiences and memories, they develop a greater degree of trust and closeness.

It is necessary to plan and participate in activities together, to make an effort to build shared memories, and to speak about and reminisce over shared experiences to share experiences and develop shared memories.

Seek professional assistance: If trust and intimacy concerns linger, professional assistance may be useful. A therapist or counselor may assist couples in identifying and resolving underlying difficulties.

In conclusion, developing trust and closeness in a relationship is critical for developing a strong, healthy connection with your spouse. Trust and intimacy are inextricably linked, and both are required for a relationship to flourish. Couples can work to build and maintain trust and intimacy in their relationship by communicating openly and honestly, being consistent and dependable, sharing vulnerabilities, showing appreciation and gratitude, resolving conflicts effectively, showing physical affection, sharing experiences and creating shared memories, and seeking professional help when necessary.

It is critical to remember that developing trust and closeness requires time and work and that it is a continuous process. It's also crucial to keep in mind that no relationship is flawless, and there will always be ups and downs. Couples may form a deep and enduring relationship by working together and being devoted to creating trust and intimacy.

It's also worth noting that trust and intimacy may mean various things to different couples, so it's important to talk and understand what trust and intimacy mean to each partner before working toward it together.

Another thing to keep in mind is that outside circumstances such as mental health, prior traumas, financial hardship, and other life events may all have an impact on trust and intimacy. So, to have a good relationship, it is critical to acknowledge and work on these external influences.

Finally, developing trust and closeness in a relationship is critical for developing a strong, healthy connection with your spouse. Couples may try to create and maintain trust and intimacy in their relationship by learning and applying the tactics suggested in this article. It's crucial to remember that developing trust and intimacy takes time and work and that it's a continuous process, but it's well worth it to form a strong and enduring bond.

The role of trust in healthy relationships

Trust is an essential component of every good relationship. It is the basis upon which all other parts of a relationship are constructed. Individuals feel comfortable and secure in their relationships when trust is established, enabling them to be vulnerable and honest with one another. Without trust, partnerships may become strained, prompting members to withdraw emotionally and eventually leading to the relationship's dissolution.

A range of activities and behaviors contribute to the development of trust. Being consistent and trustworthy in one's conduct is one of the most vital. This includes keeping commitments, being trustworthy, and acting honestly and straightforwardly. Furthermore, forgiving may be used to foster trust. Individuals who can forgive one another for errors and trespasses serve to build the relationship's trust.

Communication is also important in developing trust in a partnership. Building trust requires the ability to talk freely and honestly with one another without fear of judgment or condemnation. It's also critical to actively listen to and validate one another's emotions and viewpoints. Individuals are more prone to trust one another when they feel heard and understood.

Sharing personal facts and experiences also helps to build trust. Individuals may establish a better understanding and connection with one another when they share more of themselves. This might strengthen the relationship's feeling of trust and closeness.

Boundaries are also essential in developing trust in a relationship. Each person has their own set of limits and requirements, which must be respected and honored in the partnership. This implies that people must be prepared to compromise and make sacrifices for one another while simultaneously asserting their own needs and desires.

Furthermore, trust is established through being responsible and accepting responsibility for one's conduct. Individuals who accept responsibility for their acts indicate that they are trustworthy and reliable. It also entails admitting faults and taking measures to correct them.

Trust, on the other hand, does not develop overnight. Establishing and maintaining trust in a relationship requires time and regular work. Individuals must be patient and tolerant of one another as they seek to create trust in their relationship.

When there is trust in a relationship, people may be more honest and vulnerable with one another. They may communicate their thoughts and wants without fear of being rejected or judged. They may also lean on one another for help and understanding. Trust makes people feel safe and secure in their relationships, which leads to deeper emotional connections and stronger ties.

When trust is destroyed, though, it may be difficult to repair. It will take a lot of time and effort from both sides, and it may be impossible to rebuild the level of trust that existed before. When trust is lost, people must accept responsibility for their acts, apologize, and make restitution.

Finally, trust is an essential component of every good partnership. It makes people feel comfortable and secure, which leads to deeper emotional connections and stronger ties. Trust is created by a range of acts and behaviors, such as consistency and dependability, forgiveness, open and honest communication, sharing personal information, and respecting boundaries. However, trust does not happen immediately, and it is difficult to recover once it has been lost. Individuals must be patient and empathetic as they seek to establish trust in their relationships.

Tips for fostering intimacy and connection

A healthy and successful relationship requires the development and maintenance of intimacy and connection. Here are some pointers to help you create closeness and connection in your relationship:

Communicate freely and honestly: Communicating openly and honestly with your spouse is one of the most crucial things you can do to create closeness and connection in your relationship. This is communicating your views, emotions, and needs to your spouse while also actively listening to what they have to say.

Physical contact, such as holding hands, hugging, and kissing, may aid in the development of closeness and connection in a relationship. Make an effort to express love to your mate regularly.

Spending quality time together is vital for developing closeness and connection in a relationship. Make frequent date evenings a priority, or just set aside time each day to converse and connect.

Show thanks and appreciation: Showing gratitude and appreciation for your mate may assist to establish closeness and connection in a relationship. Tell your lover how much you appreciate them and what they do for you.

Supporting one another through tough times may assist to establish closeness and connection in a relationship. Be there for your spouse when they need you and assist them in overcoming whatever obstacles they may be experiencing.

Being truthful about your wants in a relationship is vital for developing closeness and connection. If you're unhappy in one aspect of your relationship, tell your spouse what you need to feel better and more connected.

Vulnerability: Being vulnerable with your spouse may aid in the development of intimacy and connection. Discuss your worries, anxieties, and emotions with your companion.

Empathy: Empathy for your spouse may aid in the development of intimacy and connection. Put yourself in your partner's shoes and try to comprehend their point of view.

Making time for intimacy is essential for developing closeness and connection in a relationship. Make time once a week to be intimate with your lover.

Take time to reflect and develop as a couple: Reflecting on your relationship and working on personal growth as a couple may help you establish closeness and connection. Take time to reflect on your relationship and focus on personal development together.

Be open to new ideas and diverse ways of thinking: Being open to new ideas and different ways of thinking may assist to establish closeness and connection in a relationship. Be open to new ideas and eager to attempt new things.

Work through disagreements: Conflict is unavoidable in every relationship, but how you manage disagreements may bring you closer together or rip you apart. Work through disagreements healthily and helpfully.

Show interest in each other's lives and interests: Showing interest in each other's lives and hobbies may aid in the development of closeness and connection. Spend time getting to know your partner's interests and supporting them in their activities.

Laugh and have fun together: Having a sense of humor and being able to laugh together may assist a relationship to establish closeness and connection. Have a good time and enjoy each other's company.

Demonstrate forgiveness and understanding: Demonstrating forgiveness and understanding may aid in the development of closeness and connection in a relationship. When your spouse makes a mistake, attempt to forgive them and understand their point of view.

You may develop a strong and loving partnership that will last a lifetime by following these recommendations and making a deliberate effort to cultivate intimacy and connection in your relationship. Remember that developing closeness and connection is a process that takes both partners' dedication, patience, and understanding.

Chapter 5: Dealing with Infidelity and Trust Issues

In a relationship, dealing with infidelity and trust difficulties may be very tough and hurtful. However, with the appropriate technique, these obstacles may be worked through and a better and more trustworthy connection can be built.

a. **Recognize and affirm your emotions**: It is critical to identify and validate your sentiments while coping with infidelity and trust concerns. You may be experiencing a variety of feelings, including rage, pain, betrayal, and grief. It is important to allow oneself time to digest these feelings and to experience them.

b. **Communicate freely and honestly**: When coping with infidelity and trust concerns, open and honest communication is essential. Both partners should be open to sharing their views and emotions about the problem, as well as actively listening to one another.

c. **Take responsibility**: When coping with infidelity, both parties must accept responsibility for their behavior. If one partner has cheated, they must accept responsibility and apologize for the grief they have caused. If the other spouse is to blame for the collapse of trust in the relationship, they must accept responsibility for their actions as well.

d. **Seek professional assistance**: If you are having problems dealing with infidelity and trust issues on your own, it may be beneficial to seek professional assistance. A therapist or counselor may provide advice and support as you go through this challenging period in your relationship.

Be open and honest: Following adultery, the cheating spouse must be forthcoming about their behaviors and whereabouts. This entails being upfront and honest about your whereabouts, who you've been with, and what you've been up to. This may assist to repair trust by demonstrating to the other spouse that you intend to be open and honest in the future.

e. **Be open to feedback**: It is important to be open to criticism and eager to hear the other person's point of view. This includes being open to hearing their views and emotions about what occurred, as well as taking their comments into account as you strive to reestablish trust.
f. **Invest in repairing trust**: When coping with infidelity and trust concerns, rebuilding trust is critical. This may be

accomplished by simple acts of compassion and honesty, such as being open to comments and being clear about your activities.

g. **Take a break**: Taking a break from a relationship may sometimes assist to cleanse the mind and obtain a fresh perspective. This may assist both couples in reflecting on their behaviors and emotions and determining whether or not they want to work on restoring the relationship.

h. **Forgiveness**: Dealing with infidelity and trust difficulties requires forgiveness. Both spouses must realize that forgiveness does not imply forgetting what has occurred, but rather that it is a process that enables both parties to go ahead and heal.

i. **Set clear limits**: Setting clear boundaries may aid in the rebuilding of trust in a relationship. Both parties should be clear about what they are comfortable with and what they want to get out of the relationship in the future.

j. **Please be patient**: It takes time and compassion to rebuild trust and work over infidelity and trust difficulties. Both parties must be willing to put in the time and effort required to restore the relationship.

k. **Reflect on the relationship**: Reflecting on the relationship and recognizing the underlying problems that lead to infidelity or trust difficulties might assist to prevent them from recurring.

It is important to remember that mending and restoring trust after infidelity is a process that takes time, patience, and dedication on the side of both spouses. It's also crucial to realize that everyone is unique, and some individuals may need more time to recover and move on. It is critical to remember that rebuilding trust takes time and cannot be hurried or coerced.

It's also important to recognize that infidelity isn't always the consequence of a lack of love or devotion. It may be an indication of deeper difficulties inside the relationship, such as a lack of emotional closeness, unfulfilled needs, or unresolved previous traumas. As a result, it is critical to treat these underlying concerns as part of the healing process.

When dealing with trust concerns, keep in mind that trust is earned over time by consistent acts and conduct.

Understanding the reasons behind infidelity

Infidelity, or being disloyal in a love relationship, maybe a complicated and tough topic to comprehend. There are several reasons why individuals choose to cheat on their relationships, and no one answer applies to all situations. However, some of the most typical causes for infidelity are as follows:

Unsatisfied emotional needs: A lack of emotional connection or satisfaction in the existing relationship is one of the most prominent grounds for adultery. People may cheat because they are emotionally distant from their spouse or because their emotional needs are not being addressed inside the relationship. Feeling undervalued, insignificant, or unwanted is one example.

Boredom or a need for novelty: People may cheat because they are bored or want a new experience. This might involve a desire to try something new, as well as a sense that the existing relationship has become too normal or predictable.

Infidelity is also often caused by a lack of closeness in the existing relationship. This might involve a sense that the physical component of the relationship is missing, as well as a lack of emotional intimacy between the pair.

Low self-esteem: Some individuals may cheat because they are seeking affirmation or approval from others and have low self-esteem. They may desire someone else's attention or love to increase their self-esteem and feel better about themselves.

Relationship problems: Infidelity may be an indication of deeper problems in a relationship. Lack of communication, unsolved problems, or a lack of trust may all contribute to this.

Sexual addiction: Some people cheat because they have an uncontrolled drive to participate in sexual conduct despite the negative repercussions.

People may cheat as a result of prior traumas or experiences that have harmed their capacity to develop good relationships. Previous infidelities, abuse, or a history of unstable relationships are examples of this.

Societal and cultural elements: Societal and cultural variables may both contribute to infidelity. Some cultures, for example, maybe more accepting of adultery, or individuals may be more willing to cheat if they live in a society that promotes infidelity.

Hereditary and neurological factors: Studies have shown that infidelity may have a genetic and neurological component. Certain genetic and neurological variables, according to research, may make some individuals more prone to cheat than others.

It's vital to remember that adultery is a complicated problem with various causes. A person may cheat for any of the reasons listed above, or a combination of causes may lead to infidelity.

When it comes to dealing with infidelity, both couples must understand the underlying causes of the conduct. This might include communicating openly and honestly, getting professional treatment, and addressing any underlying problems or traumas that may be contributing to the infidelity.

It's also worth noting that mending and restoring trust after infidelity is a tough and time-consuming process that needs a great deal of patience, understanding, empathy, and a desire to work through the challenges together. It's also crucial to remember that the process of reestablishing trust and repairing the relationship is unique to each partner.

To summarize, infidelity is a complicated problem with several underlying reasons. Both couples must understand the reasons for the infidelity and address any underlying problems or traumas that may be contributing to the adultery. Healing and restoring trust after infidelity is a tough and time-consuming process that needs patience, understanding, sensitivity, and a desire to work through the challenges together.

How to rebuild trust and move forward after infidelity

Rebuilding trust and moving ahead in a relationship after infidelity may be a tough and stressful process, but it is doable. Following are some measures that may be followed to help repair trust and move on following infidelity:

- **Understand the reasons for the infidelity**: It is critical to understand the reasons for the adultery to treat any underlying problems and avoid future infidelity. This might include communicating openly and honestly, obtaining professional treatment, and addressing any underlying problems or traumas that may have led to the adultery.

Take full responsibility for your acts: The individual who committed adultery must accept full responsibility for their actions and be prepared to make apologies. This involves apologizing and being prepared to go to any length to win their partner's confidence.

Effective communication is critical for re-establishing trust following infidelity. Both parties must be able to freely and honestly share their thoughts and worries, as well as be ready to listen to each other. This might include making time for conversation, being patient, and avoiding blame or criticism.

Seek professional assistance: Seeking the assistance of a therapist or counselor to work through the difficulties and give direction and support may be beneficial. A therapist may help couples acquire new communication and problem-solving skills, as well as understand and work through their emotions.

Be patient: It takes time to rebuild trust and move on after betrayal. It is critical that everyone be patient with one another and not expect problems to be settled quickly. It is critical to recognize that mending and restoring trust after infidelity is a tough and time-consuming process that involves a great deal of patience, understanding, empathy, and a desire to work through the challenges together.

Forgiveness is essential in repairing trust after betrayal. Forgiveness helps both parties to move forward from the past. Forgiveness does not imply forgetting or dismissing the infidelity; rather, it entails letting go of the anger, pain, and resentment and enabling the healing process to begin.

Work on restoring trust: Rebuilding trust is a slow and laborious task. It is critical to begin modestly to develop trust and progressively increase the amount of trust as the relationship grows. This may include restoring confidence in minor areas like punctuality, honoring commitments, and preserving transparency.

Re-establishing boundaries: It is critical for both couples to re-establish boundaries after infidelity. Setting clear standards for the relationship and addressing what is and is not appropriate conduct are examples of this.

Invest in the relationship: Rebuilding trust and moving ahead after infidelity takes time and effort from both parties. Spending quality time together, focusing on regaining trust and closeness, and taking measures to deepen the relationship may all contribute to this.

Let go of the past: It is important to let go of the past and concentrate on the present and future. Holding on to the past and obsessing about the infidelity may stymie the healing process and make moving ahead difficult. It is critical to prioritize repairing trust and going on in the relationship.

Rebuilding trust and moving ahead after infidelity is a tough and time-consuming process that involves patience, understanding, empathy, and a desire to work through the challenges together. It's also essential to remember that each relationship's process of restoring trust and moving ahead is unique, and what works for one couple may not work for another. It is critical to seek professional assistance if necessary, as well as to be patient with each other as you go through the process of restoring trust and moving ahead.

Chapter 6: Maintaining a Healthy Relationship

A good relationship requires continual work and dedication from both parties. Here are some pointers for keeping a good relationship:

Communication: The cornerstone of every good relationship is effective communication. It is critical to be open and honest with your spouse, as well as to be active and empathetically listen. This involves talking about both happy and negative emotions and figuring out how to settle disagreements.

Trust: A strong partnership requires trust. It is critical to be trustworthy and dependable, as well as honest about your behaviors and emotions. It takes time and works to build and maintain trust, and it should be a continual priority in the relationship.

Respect: It is essential to show respect for your spouse and their emotions to have a good relationship. Listening to their point of view, appreciating their thoughts, and treating them with love and understanding are all examples of this.

Spending quality time together is essential for sustaining a good relationship. This involves making time to be together without distractions like phones or work, as well as participating in activities that you both like.

Support: A successful relationship needs mutual support in both good and difficult times. This involves giving emotional support, being there for one another, and extending practical assistance as required.

Flexibility: Every relationship goes through ups and downs. It is important to be adaptive and flexible to negotiate these changes and have a good relationship.

Shared values and objectives: Having shared values and goals is essential for a good partnership. It is critical to communicate and comprehend each other's values and aims, as well as to develop methods to match them.

Self-care: It is essential to take care of oneself both physically and emotionally to sustain a successful relationship. Taking time for yourself, participating in self-care activities, and preserving your interests and hobbies are all examples of this.

Keeping the flame alive: Keeping the spark alive in a good relationship takes work. Planning date nights, experiencing new things together, and making time for romance and intimacy are all examples of this.

Growth: For a relationship to be healthy, both parties must continue to grow and develop as people. Setting personal objectives, following hobbies, and helping each other to develop and evolve are all examples of this.

Maintaining a good relationship is a continual endeavor that takes a lot of work, but it is also one of the most gratifying things you can do for yourself and your spouse. It is critical to have a common idea of what a good relationship entails and to be prepared to put in the time and effort required to make it happen. Be open and honest with each other, communicate well, trust and respect each other, make time for each other, and be ready to work on the relationship at all times. Remember that a good relationship is a two-way street, and both parties must contribute to its success.

How to set boundaries and maintain independence

Setting limits and retaining independence in a relationship is critical for both parties' health and well-being. Boundaries are the restrictions we create for ourselves and others to safeguard our physical, emotional, and mental health. Maintaining independence entails retaining our identity and the characteristics that distinguish us, even when in a partnership. Here are some pointers on how to create limits and retain independence in a relationship:

- **Express your requirements to your spouse:** It is important to communicate your demands and limits to your partner.

This involves stating what you are and are not comfortable with, as well as what you need from the relationship and your expectations. Misunderstandings and disagreements may be avoided via clear and honest communication.

- ❖ **Respect your partner's limits**: Just as you should express your boundaries, you should also respect your partner's. This involves respecting their wishes and not pressuring them to do things they do not want to do.
- ❖ **Make time for yourself**: Making time for yourself and engaging in things that you like is essential. Hobbies, interests, and

spending time with friends and family are examples of this. Having your hobbies and activities allows you to keep your independence while also bringing new ideas and energy to the partnership.

- **Prioritize your wants and well-being in the relationship**: It is critical to prioritize your own needs and well-being in the partnership. This involves establishing limits for your time, energy, and resources, as well as not ignoring your own needs to please your spouse.
- **Maintain separate funds**: Keeping your finances separate might help you maintain your independence and autonomy in the

relationship. Having your bank account, credit cards, and other financial resources is part of this.

Establishing good limits with family and friends is vital. This might involve talking with your spouse about how much time and energy you want to commit to them, as well as how much time you want to spend with them separately.

- ❖ **Be willing to compromise**: Setting limits and maintaining independence are vital, but so is being willed to compromise. This involves striking a balance between your own and your partner's requirements.
- ❖ **Seek assistance if necessary**: If you are having difficulty setting boundaries or

maintaining independence in your relationship, consulting with a therapist or counselor may be beneficial. They may provide advice and assistance in managing these challenges.

Keep in mind that limits and independence might shift over time: Relationship dynamics may change over time, so it's important to check in with yourself and your spouse frequently to ensure that your boundaries and independence remain aligned.

- **If necessary, don't be scared to terminate the relationship**: If you are unable to create limits and retain your independence in your partnership, it may be essential to terminate the connection. It is important to remember that sacrificing your well-being for the sake of a relationship is unhealthy.

In conclusion, creating boundaries and preserving independence in a partnership is critical for both partners' well-being. Clear communication, mutual respect, and a willingness to compromise are required. Keep in mind that your wants and well-being are equally as essential as your partner's and that a good partnership allows both individuals to retain their uniqueness and autonomy.

The importance of self-care and self-growth in a relationship

Maintaining a healthy and satisfying relationship requires self-care and self-growth. We are better suited to face the difficulties of being in a relationship and to be better partners when we take care of ourselves and concentrate on our growth. Here are some ways that self-care and self-development may help a relationship:

Improving communication: Self-care and self-growth may help us better understand our own needs and feelings, which can help us communicate more effectively with our spouse. We are better equipped to communicate ourselves clearly and effectively when we take the time to comprehend and process our own emotions.

Self-care and self-growth may also aid in the development of trust in a relationship. We are more likely to be trusted and appreciated if we take the time to work on ourselves and be honest with our partners about our ideas and emotions.

Stress reduction: Taking care of ourselves and focusing on our development might assist to lessen stress in a relationship. We can better manage our stress by adopting good coping strategies and self-care routines, which may assist to minimize stress in the relationship as a whole.

Self-care and self-growth may also help to increase emotional connection in a relationship. We are more likely to connect with our spouse on a deeper level when we take the time to understand our feelings and work through any obstacles.

Personal development may be encouraged in a relationship by practicing self-care and self-growth. We are more likely to be able to assist and encourage our spouses in their development path if we take the time to work on ourselves.

Managing expectations: Self-care and self-development may aid in the management of expectations in a relationship. Understanding our wants and aspirations allows us to convey them to our spouse more effectively and control any unreasonable expectations that may be generating conflict.

Self-care and self-growth may also aid in the development of relationship resilience. We are better prepared to face the obstacles and tensions that come with being in a relationship if we take care of ourselves and concentrate on our growth.

Keeping a sense of self: Self-care and self-growth may aid in keeping a feeling of self in a relationship. We may keep our uniqueness and autonomy even when in a relationship if we take the time to understand and nurture our own needs and aspirations.

Improving self-esteem: Self-care and self-growth may also boost self-esteem, which can benefit a relationship. When we invest in ourselves and recognize our value, we are more likely to be able to express ourselves in a relationship and be valued by our partners.

Encourage mutual growth: Self-care and self-development may also promote mutual growth in a partnership. We are more likely to be able to assist and encourage our spouses in their development paths if we take the time to work on ourselves.

Maintaining a healthy and satisfying relationship requires self-care and self-growth. We are better equipped to handle the challenges that come with being in a relationship if we work on ourselves and understand our own needs and emotions. We are better equipped to communicate more effectively, build trust, reduce stress, promote emotional intimacy, manage expectations, build resilience, maintain a sense of self, improve self-esteem, and encourage mutual growth. Remember to arrange a time for self-care and personal development activities, and discuss your requirements for self-care and personal growth with your spouse. This will help kids realize the significance of these activities in their life, as well as motivate them to take care of themselves. It may also assist to build limits and independence within the relationship, which is essential for sustaining a healthy and successful connection.

Some self-care activities that may be implemented into a partnership are as follows:

Exercise and physical exercise: Physical activity regularly may assist to decrease stress, and enhance mood, and general well-being.

Meditation and mindfulness activities may help you concentrate while also reducing stress and anxiety.

Spending time alone: It is essential to have time alone to rejuvenate and contemplate.

Hobbies and interests: Hobbies and interests may provide enjoyment and a feeling of achievement.

Personal development activities that may be implemented into a partnership are as follows:

Reading and learning new topics might assist to broaden one's knowledge and viewpoint.

Setting and achieving personal objectives may assist to boost confidence and a feeling of purpose.

Therapy or counseling may assist in working through personal challenges and improving communication skills.

It's also vital to remember that reestablishing trust after adultery requires time and work on the side of both parties. Seeking counseling or therapy jointly to work through the challenges and create a strategy for regaining trust may be beneficial. Setting limits, being truthful with one another, and accepting responsibility for previous behaviors are all examples of this.

Furthermore, keep in mind that relationships are continually developing and take continuing work to sustain. This implies that self-care and personal development activities should be included in the relationship regularly, rather than as a one-time effort.

Overall, self-care and self-development are vital for a successful and satisfying partnership. We are better equipped to handle the challenges that come with being in a relationship if we work on ourselves and understand our own needs and emotions. We are better equipped to communicate more effectively, build trust, reduce stress, promote emotional intimacy, manage expectations, build resilience, maintain a sense of self, improve self-esteem, and encourage mutual growth. Furthermore, creating boundaries and a feeling of independence within the relationship may assist to maintain a healthy balance and guarantee that both partners can continue to develop and expand as individuals while remaining connected as a pair.

Conclusion: Empowering Yourself to Create a Strong and Lasting Relationship

Creating a solid and long-lasting relationship demands a significant amount of work and dedication from both sides. However, to have a healthy and satisfying connection, it is equally necessary to empower yourself and take charge of your happiness and well-being.

Setting firm boundaries is one of the most essential things you can do to empower yourself in a relationship. This entails defining what is and is not acceptable conduct from your spouse and being able to express yourself and effectively convey these boundaries. This might involve things like establishing time restrictions for spending time together or addressing communication and intimacy standards. You take charge of your wants and desires by creating clear boundaries and ensuring that they are respected and addressed inside the partnership.

Maintaining a feeling of independence is another crucial component of empowering yourself in a relationship. This includes having your interests, hobbies, and activities outside of the partnership. It is important to take time for yourself and to follow your objectives and dreams. You are less likely to become too reliant on your spouse if you keep a feeling of independence, and you can better maintain a healthy balance in the relationship.

To have a solid and enduring relationship, it is also necessary to take care of yourself emotionally and physically. Taking time for self-care activities such as exercise, meditation, and counseling is part of this. It also entails being able to understand and regulate your own emotions, as well as successfully communicating them to your spouse. You may build more robust and secure relationships by taking care of yourself emotionally and physically.

Communication is another important aspect of empowering yourself in a relationship. It is critical to be able to convey your wants and aspirations, as well as actively listen to and comprehend your partner's point of view. This involves the ability to conduct tough talks and resolve issues healthily and productively. By speaking properly, you may increase trust and intimacy in your relationship and develop a stronger bond with your spouse.

It is equally critical to focus on your personal development and improvement. Reading, gaining new skills, or following your aims and dreams are examples of this. You can contribute fresh views and energy to the relationship by continuing to develop and evolve as an individual, and you can better support your spouse in their personal growth by continuing to grow and evolve as an individual.

Being honest with yourself about what you want and need in a relationship is also part of self-empowerment. It's important to be realistic about your expectations and objectives with yourself and your spouse and to have open and honest dialogues about them. You may develop a more true and happy relationship by being honest with yourself and your spouse.

Finally, keep in mind that a successful and enduring relationship needs continual work and dedication. This entails being willing to invest the time and energy necessary to improve yourself and your relationship, as well as to continue to develop and progress as a pair. It also entails being able to forgive and let go of previous errors, as well as developing resilience and emotional intelligence to deal with obstacles that may arise in the relationship.

Overall, empowering yourself in a relationship entails taking charge of your happiness and well-being, as well as actively trying to build healthy and long-lasting relationships. You can create a healthy and fulfilling relationship by setting clear boundaries, maintaining your independence, taking care of yourself emotionally and physically, communicating effectively, working on personal growth and development, being honest with yourself and your partner, and committing to an ongoing effort.

www.ingramcontent.com/pod-product-compliance
Lightning Source LLC
LaVergne TN
LVHW012100160826
845678LV00014B/2889

9798375300474